STUDY GUIDE

FOR NOVEL TWO

*Novel Edition

ISBN: 978-0-557-06495-3

Fiction

ISBN: 978-0-557-06495-3

STUDY GUIDE

NOVEL TWO

*Novel Edition

By

Neebeeshaabookway

*For Use With The Jake Smith Ranch Series

~*~ TABLE OF CONTENTS ~*~

*http://go.neebeeshaabookway.com (free seizure info flyers)

INTRODUCTION TO BOOK'S PURPOSE:

INTRODUCTION TO BOOK'S PURPOSE:

Hey there and hello!

Author note:

The purpose of this FIRST section
is to give any of you pre-teens a preview of what to expect
and help you in your decision as to be reading this book—or—
on how you may share and use it for head injury awareness
and seizure awareness, along with,
tongue-loss awareness-issues.

*Some of you may even have family members, or friends that have lost part of their tongue, or their voice box, due to cancer—or have had a serious head injury from an accident—perhaps this book will help you understand the problems that they face, after you read these novels.

Thank you for your time, courtesy, and study, of this novel.
God bless, Neebeeshaabookway (Lizzy)

GOOD REASONS TO LEARN

GOOD REASONS TO LEARN:

More-and-more folks are finding themselves in the situation of having family members that have head injuries. The obstacles that folks, both with the injury, and those in the family, seek to deal with, are very strenuous, both mentally and physically.

This four-novel series about Jake and his twin Jade, seeks to show through an adventure in their lives—"fiction"—though based as close as possible, to facts, that:

1. Friends and family make a <u>vast</u> difference as one *heals*.
2. There is <u>still</u> a hope for joy and love to surround the home, through patience and learning "the trail".
3. And—that a fiction story can encourage folks to go out and learn more truth on these issues—and then, this book will have thankfully been *part* of some new *learning*, in your life, that led you to more learning tools.
4. And—hopefully it will be inspiration to you and your family, NOT to give up, while tackling your hard trail.

IN THIS SECOND NOVEL:

IN THIS SECOND NOVEL:

---

1. You will see how Jake has Sofia come to live at the ranch—though in separate quarters of the house. He now courts her to be his wife—giving her a chance to "practice" with his injuries, and learn from Jade.

2. You will see some of the troubles a man runs into with his self-esteem when he only wishes to be his very best, for his gal. You will see how Sofia responds to this.

3. You will see how good friends and buddies are needed to "fish one out of trouble"—Jake seems to find more than his share, due to his injury—just by being a hero, again.

4. You get to see how one twin is now ready to accept a new person in the other twin's life.

5. You learn that due to physical injuries (though not always), marriage plans *can* mess-up—but it is the goal and keeping of it, that counts—even though for Jake, it proves to be hard.

6. You get to see how one has many personal inner-feelings to deal with, if one wants to conquer injuries, fears, doubts and obstacles, and—only a partner of equal stamina, and insight, and goals, will understand this job.

HOPEFULLY YOU ARE CURIOUS NOW:

HOPEFULLY YOU ARE CURIOUS NOW:

Here are a few things you can do now as you read the book, if you've chosen to buy any of the novels of the JAKE SMITH RANCH SERIES and it's short-stories of insight—or if it is just school work:

1. Find out what you can learn through the library, or, online, about head injuries (TBI).

2. Find out what you can learn through the library, or, online, about epilepsy (seizures).

3. Find out about tongue-loss. Many folks that suffer from this, have faced cancer, in the mouth, throat, or tongue-areas, and not as an injury such as Jake's. Yet, in rare incidences, folks have really lost parts (or nearly all) of their tongue in other ways.

- I -

WHO ELSE MAY LIKE THIS BOOK?

TWINS.

WHO ELSE MAY LIKE THIS BOOK?

TWINS.

This book is not only for those facing head injury issues, or any of the specific ones that Jake faces. This book has many benefits for those that are twins.

When a twin finds someone to marry, it most likely will become a three-fold team—if the twinship was a close one. A new member can either balance or unbalance a previously well-working team of two. Jade and Sofia have a talk, and by their relationship you will learn—twins with insight, can see this new challenge through.

This is "your" twin book, with twin heroes, one that you will truly understand. The twin-type-trail takes the right friends to understand it. This book is a good tool.

- II -

WHO ELSE MAY LIKE THIS BOOK?

COWBOY RANCHERS.

WHO ELSE MAY LIKE THIS BOOK?

COWBOY RANCHERS.

YEP—Jake and his gang are ranchers from Montana. Well, seems they have moved up from Texas; though when quite *young*—but you get the drift. Getting back out into working a trail-drive, or herding animals on any ranch, lead to seeing *other* cowboys. How does one handle ranch-work when one can't talk? Folks must learn Jake's new signed language—a language that some guys may just not take to.

Situations to conquer are not only in the home, but due to *working situations* on other ranches during emergencies; this can turn into hard things to "rein in" to control.

So—this second book, still follows the ol' cowboy theme—showing some rescue work, too, and respect to Jake's new gal.

- III -

WHO ELSE MAY LIKE THIS BOOK?

RODEO FOLKS.

WHO ELSE MAY LIKE THIS BOOK?

RODEO FOLKS.

Jake and his buddies, and even their families, have all come from the rodeo scene—teaching them not to be quitters.

A few situations in this book, keep one *remembering* from which line of work, these ol' cowboy-buddies have come from.

Their rodeo-riding is all done now, though, as Jake is their main focus in life now—but some of his buddies use their skill, to rescue him, due to an unforeseen, but exposed woe; they *rope* the wrong-doer.

As any good team, the victory becomes theirs—and all due to a display of team-roping. Seems you just can't take the rodeo out of the ol' cowboy—especially in solving troubles.

- IV -

WHO ELSE MAY LIKE THIS BOOK?

FOLKS THAT KNOW OF GOD'S HELP.

WHO ELSE MAY LIKE THIS BOOK?

FOLKS THAT KNOW OF GOD'S HELP.

First-off, if you do not know how God can help you through your life—do not feel the book is not for you. God is moving in behind the scenes and YOU may not even know it!

The Jake Smith Ranch Series, does show examples of this, and God gets Jake through some hard times during his courting-season—thus bringing him safely to the alter to marry his gal.

FOR those of you that DO know of how God moves through one's life, and how He is a great "restorer", you will take joy in seeing the story-line of God's ways revealed in this fiction book—God honors marriage, and makes a way for Jake to succeed.

When this book ends, there is a feeling of the new path that will unfold, and how it well be well-worth the hard trail that led to it. It may be hard to work a marriage after injury—but—it is possible, by God's grace.

As you read this book, may you pray for help and grace for your injured family members—or for those that you know, or may not know, that are suffering from these very hard issues presented in this book.

Perhaps very similar issues have prevented someone from marrying—or—worse yet, perhaps they have caused a marriage to fall into ruin. Pray for new steps in someone's lives today—new steps of hope. As a good friend, you may need to be there until this hard time passes.

And may God richly bless you
as you seek him.

*And—thank you for taking a few moments to study-up on a bit of notes as to this book being a learning tool. Pass the word, around, about overcoming, though love.

BEGIN:
STUDY-GUIDE QUESTIONS

(In Four Parts)

- USER GUIDE -

Use the page-title to start-off the questions, when the questions are NOT A FULL SENTENCE.

PART ONE - DO YOU REMEMBER DETAILS?

1. What two reasons caused Jake to leave the trail-drive? Who is Marsh?

2. After Jake's seizure in the field, what "showed him'" that he suffered one?

3. Why won't Jake go in the Emergency Vehicle—what finally makes him go?

4. What does Jake hear after he wakes up at home? How and why is he stuck?

5. What did Sofia say a good gal and good dog would do?

6. When Jake goes back to the hospital, who has a talk with Sofia, and why?

7. After the 4th of July, what will Sofia do again? For how long?

8. What does the gang plan to do on the 4th of July? With who-all?

9. What does Jake go to do first? What goes wrong? Why did this happen?

10. Who comes to help Jake? What else goes wrong? Why did Ray need Lenny?

11. What happens to Jake next, at Ray's? What triggered this to happen?

12. Who do they call in Texas; why did they need to? Why didn't they wait?

13. Why did Jake earnestly still want to go to Johnny's? Who-all is still there?

14. What does Sofia do with the ladder and why? Who helps her?

15. What happens when Jake needs to take a bath?

16. What does Jake find in the dirt, one night, with Sofia? What's it mean?

17. At night, during coffee, what 2 serious things does Jade share with Sofia?

18. What happens at the bar, with Jake, during the twins' birthday bash?

19. What 3 main things is Jake thinking about, at this time?

20. What does Jade finally start doing at the bar, and why? What happens?

22. How old are the twins? Who else recently had birthdays?

23. What important thing does Jake do at home? Does he succeed? Why?

24. What does Sofia do with Harper, and why? What else does she do?

25. What does Jade have to help Jake do, and what does she make him do?

26. While Jake goes to the hospital again, what does Galena think about?

27. What 2 reasons does Ray come to visit and surprise Jake about?

28. What does Jake agree to do for Ray? What does Jake not do for Honor?

29. What shocks Jake, in the kitchen? What happens? What does Jake do?

30. What do blowing leaves make Jake dwell on? What does he tell Jade?

31. What surprise does Jade and Stoney bring in from the snow, to share?

32. What does Jake seriously then have a need to do? Why? What's Sofia say?

33. What 2 visitors come to the ranch? How did Jake shock them? Why?

34. What did Jade use to present Jake in a "good light" to Telly?

35. What is the Barn Owl picnic, and why? What are Sofia's 2 birthdays?

36. What do Vin and Carl do to Marsh, and what is their reasoning?

37. What happens when Jake rescues Marsh? How does Jade find out?

38. What does Stoney do to Jake, at the bachelor party? Who frees Jake?

39. What happens to Sofia during the wedding? How does Jake do his vows?

40. Who shows Jake how to carry Sofia over the threshold? How is this done?

41. What did Jake ask Sofia to do, that made him run away? Where did he go?

42. Where do Jake and Sofia sleep? Who watches over them, 'til morning?

43. What was the one last wound? Why is gang still gone?

44. What does Sofia hide from Jake, and why? What does Jake think, at first?

45. What is the last gift Jade gives to Sofia? When does she open it?

46 – Make up your own question- write it in:

PART TWO - DO YOU REMEMBER KEY ISSUES?

1. **TAKE ABOUT:** reasons why Jake didn't want to go on trail-ride?

2. reasons why Jake felt he was not fitting in, and why he left the ride?

3. how Stoney takes care to protect Jake, when Marsh ridicules him?

4. Jake's decision to leave camp, alone, and the dangers?

5. Jake's embarrassment at being "muffled" and in bed, full of tubes?

6. Sofia learning how to care for Jake's eating issues?

7. Sofia, learning Jake keeps *watch* over Stoney, due to Stoney's guilt?

8. Jake (lost after Marsh attacked him) and how it affects his plans?

9. Jake's characters, as to the word, "promise" and why he was so sad?

10. how drunk-deeds affects many more lives, than just the one drunk's?

11. Jake's song for Sofia, and the song that joins Jake and Jade?

12. Jade's protective watch of Jake, at their birthday, and her deeds?

13. Jake's thoughts on trying to re-propose to Sofia, after the seizure?

14. Sofia's acceptance of Jake, and marring him, after being part of this?

15. how Jake and tack-sheds, and lassos-issues haunt him?

16. Ray's test of friendship, when he needs Jake's help with a horse?

17. the reasons that Jake shared his stickered-package with Ray?

18. Jake's stubbornness to Honor, as to trail-rides coming on his ranch?

19. why Jake's taped-voice was so powerful, he had a change of heart?

20. why Jake was pondering so hard over his last spoken words?

22. Jake's conscience pushing him to face Sofia's folks, for her *hand?*

23. how a rescue was all it took to warm Emma to Jake?

24. how giving *links* the heart, and how Telly was joined to respect Jake?

25. why Sofia was torn-up about others wanting to share her birthday?

26. why new traditions, such as the Barn Owl picnic, can heal wounds?

27. why cards or gestures of love, from Jake, were so special?

28. Jake getting overwhelmed in a store, and why it got so much worse?

29. Jake's isolation before the police, and how compassion helped him?

30. if Marsh learned a lesson, and how this affected Jake's his buddies?

31. Jake's choice to rescue Marsh, and what it involved then, and later?

32. why Jade had learned the hard way, about Jake's hero-deeds?

33. how Jake solves his wedding vows, now that he can't communicate.

34. Jake's reason for not enjoying the bachelor joke for very long?

35. Jade's way to get the whole town to share Jake's last bachelor days?

36. Jake's tradition before the wedding, and how his hands affected it?

37. why Sofia was so concerned about what to get married in?

38. Jake's surprise songs for Sofia, and how this drew them closer?

39. Jake and a deep need to feel normal again, and why Sofia helped?

40. Jake's "lost feeling" making painful memories, instead of good one?

41. the gang all getting involved to help Jake and Sofia? How and why?

42. why Stoney made Jade wait, before she ran to Jake's aid (in corral)?

43. Jake's need to face the round corral alone, after his memory-pain?

44. Jade's need to talk with Sofia about Jake's voice, and, the tape?

45. the deep issues that are learned about Jade, from her poem?

46 – Make up your own question- write it in:

PART THREE - DO YOU REMEMBER NEW HOPE?

1. **WHAT KIND OF NEW HOPE CAME?** by Matt not doing the trail-drive?

2. by Jake leaving the trail-drive—what good did this do for insight, for Sofia?

3. from Jade testing Sofia, and allowing her to be involved in Jake's needs?

4. from Jake's hospital check-up, after his recent seizure?

5. from Matt and Sofia's temporary job-switch. What new "addition" came?

6. from the attack on Jake, as he pondered under the stars?

7. when Vin and Carl found out that Marsh worked for them now?

8. when Jake saw what was done to Marsh, in public, at Vin and Carl's ranch?

9. when Jake got a sweet-heart to marry, and why is this such a huge step?

10. when Sofia's birthday was made on Valentine day?

11. when Jake dared help Marsh with the stray cows, instead of ignoring him?

12. by Jake rescuing Marsh, when Marsh was so afraid he was going to die?

13. when Jake threw rocks at Marsh's waiting partner?

14. concerning Marsh's accident, and his family-life's future?

15. when Jade challenged Jake to face Sofia—after his ruined his proposal?

16. when he DID try again, what did he learn?

17. when Jake went out in the public, during festival time?

18. when Jake rescued the deer, and made a spectacle of himself?

19. when Jake forced himself to meet Sofia's folks?

20. when Telly heard Jake's voice, by Jade's tape?

22. concerning Telly's thoughts now, for Sofia's future?

23. with the Barn Owl picnic, for both Jake and Sofia?

24. when reestablishing his connection to Robert?

25. when Jade exposes Sofia's birthday?

26. when Sofia shared her wedding dilemma, and her wedding dress story?

27. when Jade talked-out her woe, about Lyle, to Sofia?

28. when Sofia had her New Year talk with Jake, under the stars?

29. when Jake shared his new signature, for Sofia, at Valentine's Day?

30. when Matt finally knew what Jake wanted, during the bachelor party?

31. when Stoney showed Jake the bike, after the wedding?

32. when Stoney and Matt confronted Jake, after he ran out on Sofia?

33. when Jake faced his deeds, in thought, as to his honeymoon disaster?

34. when Sofia fell on the kitchen floor in dismay, in front of Jade?

35. when Jade rebuked Sofia, in the bedroom. What did Jade say, and why?

36. when Sofia found the tape of Jake's voice and played it, for herself?

37. when Jake faced the round corral, on his honeymoon night?

38. from the wild honeymoon—what did it expose? Why was it hidden before?

39. when Jake and Sofia shared the photo album of Jake's family?

40. after Sofia fell, during her wedding-walk, on the driveway?

41. concerning the bad weather, and their soon-coming wedding?

42. when the "mike" was still on, during Jake's vows?

43. as to Mr. Baker's keg of cider, from the myth?

44. due to the quite-time, between Jade and Sofia, *after* the photo-book time?

45. when Sofia opened and read her gift from Jade?

46 – Make up your own question- write it in:

PART FOUR - WHAT WOULD YOU DO?

1. **OR, HOW WOULD YOU FEEL?** if you couldn't speak-up for yourself, *ever*?
2. if you had to coach folks with a whistle, and no words?
3. about riding through the hills, if you had seizures? Is it worth the risk?
4. if you were Jake, would you have tried to stick it out, and go to Rays?
5. if you were known to take out IV tubes, would you be upset, with mitts on?
6. about strong forms of medication, and needing to take it every day?
7. by watching the stars at night? What things do you think about?
8. if you had to break a promise? What is the hardest one you ever had?
9. if your gal was waiting, would you have called Texas later? Why didn't Jake?
10. could you be as patient as Jake's buddies are with him?
11. if you had to be patient all night for a friend? What are 2 key issues, to it?
12. if you couldn't go out in public with your family? Have you ever been lost?
13. if you had to rescue a little child, would you be afraid to do this? Why?
14. about inventing new ways to communicate, or write? Would it really help?
15. if you were told you had a seizure, would you trust anyone to help you?
16. if you had a seizure on a date?—would you want to see that date again?
17. if you had to try to save someone's life, and you could fail? How'd Jake feel?
18. if you were a hero; would you be shocked to see your picture in the paper?
19. if the neighborhood bully needed to be rescued? What would you do?
20. if you had not been able to use your hands for a week—and couldn't talk?
22. if you had bad head aches all the time, and had to plan a work agenda?
23. if you had damage in your leg or arm, would you still plan your wedding?

24. if you couldn't talk, would you want to hear tapes of your voice, played?

25. if you were ganged-up-on, like Jake was, by Marsh? Or by a cousin?

26. if your buddies were drunk all the time? Would you drive with them?

27. about making a roof garden? Would it be worth all the work?

28. while seeing someone have a seizure; what if they acted strange?

29. would you laugh at your mother, sister, brother or father, if *they* had one?

30. if your folks, or grandparents had cancer and lost part of their tongue?

31. could or would you be patient, when they tried to talk to you?

32. would you finally ignore them, because it is too much work to understand?

33. if someone was *confused* from a head injury, and kept *repeating* things?

34. would you laugh; *call them retarded*? Do you know what retarded means?

35. if you heard someone call anyone retarded? Would you teach them truth?

36. would you be able to say, people aren't retarded, but their brain *can* be?

37. Jake's brain had retarded areas; can you honor such folks, as his friends did honor, him? Would you not want to, because your friends would laugh at you? Brains are fragile, yours can "*break*" just as well as anyone else's.

38. if you couldn't go buy whatever you liked? Who would you trust to do it?

39. if you were severely injured, would you work hard to get well, like Jake?

40. if you saved your friend's life—would you later be mad, if you were *hurt*?

41. if each year you had a bad "memory" to face? What help change this?

42. about meeting your gal's/guy's folks, or the father, only—or the mother?

43. if all went wrong for the meeting, and you ended up dirty, like Jake?

44. if you had to start your whole life over again, and it was twice as hard now?

45. if your courtship had serious health issues, would you want to quit?

46 – Make up your own question- write it in:

SCRIPTURE HELP THAT APPLIES, IF WANTED.

Romans 10:13
For whosoever shall call upon the name of the Lord shall be saved.

Timothy 4:18
**And the Lord shall deliver me from every evil work,
and will preserve me unto his heavenly kingdom:
to whom be glory for ever and ever. Amen.**

Philippians 4:13
I can do all things through Christ that strengthens me.

Romans 10:11
For the scripture saith, Whosoever believeth on him shall not be ashamed.

Acts 19:2
**He said unto them, Have you received the Holy Ghost since you believed?
And they said unto him, We have not so much as heard
whether there be any Holy Ghost.**

James 5:16b
The effectual fervent prayer of a righteous man availeth much.

May God bless you – **Thank you so very much for reading THE JAKE SMITH RANCH SERIES!**

FROM: THE HOLY BIBLE

The King James Version
The World Publishing Company

Fiction

ISBN: 978-0-557-06495-3

www.ingramcontent.com/pod-product-compliance
Ingram Content Group UK Ltd.
Pitfield, Milton Keynes, MK11 3LW, UK
UKHW041836200726
13854UKWH00003BA/1173